Target: Focus
20 Strategies Guaranteed to Boost Concentration, Promote Drive and Live The Dream

Veronica Korres

All content contained in this book is under copyright protection. Use of any portion of this book without the author's written and expressed consent is prohibited and publishable by applicable law.

Copyright © 2021 Veronica Korres
All rights reserved.
ISBN-13: 9798547481147

This book honors Adonai J. Jireh and
Yehoshua Hamashiach.
My life. My inspiration.

Contents

INTRODUCTION 1
STRATEGIES 3
Be Clear on The Vision And Objectives......................4
Prioritize Your Day...6
Perform Easy Tasks Early 8
Do The Bare Minimum 10
Visualize In Reverse..12
Manage your Internal Distractions.............................14
Remove External Distractions....................................16
Avoid Roadblocks 18
Improve Discipline 19
Keep Your Momentum In Overdrive..........................21
Avoid Multitasking..23
Practice Meditation 24
Exercise Regularly 26
Create A "To-Do" List..27
Latte or Matcha?..28
Take Frequent Breaks...30

Say Yes to Mozart 32

Train The Mental Muscle 33

Stare At A Distant Object 35

Sleep Sweetly 37

CONCLUSION 38

ACTION STEP WORKSHEETS 39

Be Clear on The Vision And Objectives 40

Vision Objectives 41

Prioritize Your Day 42

Perform Easy Tasks Early 43

Do The Bare Minimum 44

Avoid Roadblocks 45

Improve Discipline 46

Keep Your Momentum In Overdrive 47

Exercise Regularly 48

Create A "To-Do" List 49

INTRODUCTION

You'll have a different perspective on life once you realize the value of time. Most individuals waste time up until the penny drops, and the scary part is that they do it without even realizing it. It gets ingrained in their everyday lives, and they develop habits unaware.

Learning to stay focused is a difficult objective to achieve. You sit at your computer most days, eager to get some work done. All right, let's do this, you say to yourself. You navigate to Word or Google Drive and start a new document. You have a general notion of the tasks at hand, but how do you continue?

You scribble a few words but can't seem to remain focused. Then you think, I should do something enjoyable to wake myself up. You go to Facebook and spend 20 minutes there. Then there's an hour spent aimlessly viewing YouTube videos. Lunch will be over before you realize it, and the day will be halfway through.

Does this sound like you? Remember that it doesn't have to be like this. All you have to do now is concentrate on finishing this book to learn how to avoid being distracted.

But, before we get into the recommendations, keep in mind that avoiding distraction is difficult. It isn't easy to keep focused when you have to work for long periods, yet some people can do so. Why them and not you, one could wonder.

Furthermore, likely, you were never taught how to concentrate. In class, if your thoughts strayed and you found yourself staring out the window, your instructor was probably annoyed, but they didn't fix it by teaching you how to focus; they just expected it to happen naturally. Unfortunately, that is just not possible, especially in today's world of distractions.

Because everyone is on their own, it's up to you to figure out how to master your focus. That's why these practical pointers exist, so you may finally stay focused and on track with your goals.

STRATEGIES

Veronica Korres

Be Clear on The Vision And Objectives

As you learn how to avoid distractions, it's critical to start with a strong foundation for your attention. Determine why you need to concentrate in the first place. Do you have an important presentation at work that you need to prepare for next week? Would you like to learn how to play the guitar? And need to concentrate for an hour every day while practicing?

Determining your final objective will assist you in devoting yourself to learning how to focus. Knowing why we need to keep focused will help push us through these difficult and tiresome aspects of achieving our objectives. That's when our capacity to concentrate gets tested and when it's most required.

ACTION STEP: Jot down on a piece of paper the overreaching vision. Create a vision board including words and images that represent the vision. There may be more than one vision on the board. For instance, a photo of a Ph.D. diploma can co-exist on a vision board alongside an image of a completed mural representing the most expansive mural ever painted by one artist in the downtown art district. There are different types of vision. Both, however, can be accomplished. But how? Aren't these big lofty goals that take an incredible amount of time? Yes, they are. And that brings us to the next step.

Break down your visions into objectives. It is imperative to keep a vision board where it is visible every day. Review the vision board, choose an image or word on the board, and write the objective of that image or word. For instance, the Ph.D. diploma image represents earning a Ph.D. degree. Likewise, the mural image represents painting the mural in the downtown art district. Having these objectives written down helps clarify the goal and will serve as clarity for the next step.

Prioritize Your Day

How successfully do you think your ability to focus will be if you had 20 things to do every day?

If you're too disorganized, you won't perform those things with elegance. If you want to understand how not to become distracted, you must first break it down to its most basic components.

Limit yourself to only performing two or three critical activities every day. It's everything you'll need to start working toward your objectives. Slower is preferable to quitting too soon because you took on too much. In the end, this is healthier for your mental health since you'll be able to watch yourself progressing without becoming distracted.

ACTION STEP: Grab a planner or journal and write down the top 2 - 3 critical tasks that must be accomplished for the next day, week, or month. This step will enable you to focus on those tasks only and not become burdened with other non-essential duties that could cause burnout.

Perform Easy Tasks Early

To ensure that you complete those 2 to 3 activities, start them early so that you can stay focused on the work without getting overwhelmed. Getting a jump on those tasks tells your brain you're already planning how to accomplish goals as soon as you wake up.

It's difficult, but putting it off until later invites distraction. Unexpected emails, social media, a kid who needs your attention, or coworkers who require assistance will all serve as distractions. All of this might sap your willpower and make it difficult to concentrate on the work at hand.

ACTION STEP: Set an alarm for 3 am. Early rising helps calm the inner man and helps with focus. Grab the planner or journal and review those required 2 - 3 tasks. Perform the simplest parts of those tasks before other distractions start. Lessening the stress of completing those tasks is wise and makes for a happier day.

Do The Bare Minimum

Seeing a goal as an enormous, giant accomplishment is a simple way to destroy your focus. Most objectives will take a few weeks to months to complete, and knowing this might make it seem like it would take an eternity.

One of two things happens as a result of this:

➡ Motivation diminishes because the objective is too lofty; or

➡ It becomes a daydream about its completion.

Both are bad for your attention and might be an issue when focusing on the larger picture or employing visualization.

Instead, concentrate on performing the bare minimum of work.

ACTION STEP: Break objectives down into smaller goals. Long-range goals can take weeks or months, while short-range goals can take up to a week. Painting a mural on the side of a 50-foot building can't be done in a day. But, breaking down the steps to accomplish smaller tasks in completing the mural can be done daily. And, remember to work on 2 - 3 tasks only.

Visualize In Reverse

Visualization methods might occasionally cause more harm than good. There is, however, a method to utilize visualization, and that is to visualize oneself working.

Champion runners, who generally work backward, employ this method to great success. They first envision themselves winning, and then they reverse the process, feeling and picturing each step back to the start.

Imagine yourself performing a tiny fraction of the work at hand. It is a faster and more meaningful method to apply this.

What should you do, for example, if you need to practice your guitar, but it's across the room (let's assume maximal laziness for the sake of this example)?

Consider standing for a moment (really, think of the sensation of getting up, and then do it). It will be simple to act on that sensation if you have envisioned, pictured, and felt the act of rising.

Then, repeat the visualizing process at each stage until you have the guitar in your hands and are playing it. Visualizing makes the actions real. Your brain is engaged in the activity, therefore, preparing your body for the event. All that is left to do is put this strategy into action whenever you need to concentrate.

ACTION STEP: Visualize doing the tasks for today before actually moving to perform the first step. For example, visualize the mural completed! It's beautiful! Then, visualize picking up the tracing chalk, climbing the scaffolding, and drawing the outline on the side of the building. This technique prepares your body and focuses your mind on the task at hand.

Manage your Internal Distractions

Internal distractions are one culprit from which there is no escape. This distraction is the worst; manage them in such a way as to lower their impact on concentration. To learn how not to become distracted, you must find techniques to prepare your mind for work and easy strategies to keep it from wandering to non-essential ideas.

Bravo if you have a personal workplace approach to prepare your mind for work. If you work in the same spot every day, your mind will link that spot with job-related ideas.

Make sure you leave your workstation when you take a break. Let your thoughts run wild for a few moments to unwind.

Deadlines are also beneficial in this situation. Because you have an approaching deadline, this strategy might assist in preventing your mind from straying.

You will regulate your internal distractions all of the time if you can strengthen your concentration muscle.

But, in the end, having some traction is all it takes to silence those unwelcome ideas. Rather than focusing within, concentrate on getting something done. You will notice that all of your thoughts are focused on completing your work.

ACTION STEP: Set deadlines for the tasks at hand today. Once work has begun, be sure to move away from the workspace area from time to time for a mental break. Think about wild events or people that bring happiness to mind to recharge and refocus.

Remove External Distractions

This suggestion is a little easier since it just needs you to move away from items that are distracting you physically.

Turn off the television or work in another room if it is bothering you. If your children are shouting and playing, consider getting up and going to work before they do. In the habit of constantly checking your phone? Power down or mute the ring. Break the habit of consistently checking your phone.

Although it is typically apparent what you should do, you should not disregard this piece of advice.

ACTION STEP: It is so important to move away from distractions. Anything can become a distraction. Working in an office? Concentration shot? Move into an empty cubicle or an unoccupied conference room and shut the door. If neither of these options is feasible, try air pods or earbuds if there is no other way to drown out the office noise. Stream your favorite music or TV show. Is your phone consistently ringing? Turn it off or mute it until the task is complete.

Work from home? Try to work in a room with a door away from the family activity. Is the neighbor's dog barking a little too much? Shut the window. Turn on music or stream your favorite TV show to help drown out this distraction. But, keep it low or else run the risk of losing concentration.

Avoid Roadblocks

A unique tip not mentioned often; if you get into a roadblock in your job, put it aside and return to it later as you learn how to stay focused. Concentrate your efforts on how you can continue to work mindlessly at all costs. All this implies is that you should start with simple portions.

You may return to the more difficult sections later, and ideally, it will have come to you, or you will have gained enough momentum that working on it will not break your attention.

ACTION STEP: Stumped on how to proceed? It's a roadblock or a blockage in concentration and workflow. Break down the task at hand into steps. Whatever step is causing the roadblock, skip it. Perform other parts of the job and come back to the roadblock step last. Many times the roadblock step has turned into a hump at the end that's easy to accomplish.

Improve Discipline

You may enhance your general discipline by doing a few focus exercises.

The first is meditation, which is essentially a practiced definition of concentration and a fantastic way to improve your attention, de-stress, and get more control over your emotions.

The Pomodoro method is the second exercise, which requires you to set a timer to measure how much time you spend on a job. These are essentially focused sprints, with a substantial rest in between. Each interval enhances your capacity to stay concentrated when it counts most, assisting you in learning how to stay focused in the long run.

ACTION STEP: Learn to meditate. Think of a quote that resonates and is meaningful. Rehearse it over and over in your mind; eyes closed. Spend about 20 minutes rehearsing. With eyes open, notice breath and heart rate. Both should be significantly slower, mind cleared, and focus regained.

To try method number 2, grab your phone and find the timer feature. Set it for 25 minutes while starting the task. When the alarm rings, take a 5-minute break. Then repeat. When 4 sessions like these are complete, take a 15 - 30 minute break and repeat until the job is completed. Use this method to finish the job, learn focus, and improve speed and accuracy each time. Read more about this technique at https://todoist.com/productivity-methods/pomodoro-technique.

Keep Your Momentum In Overdrive

Momentum acts as a disciplinary lubricant, making it easier to keep to goals. And why we must never stop working towards our goals. Otherwise, we will lose momentum and rely on discipline to get back on track (not an easy thing to do).

It means we must accomplish something that moves us closer to our objectives every day (yes, even weekends and holidays).

Assuming you wish to work as a freelance writer, for example, compose one solitary pitch over the weekend. Even on Christmas Day, if you want to get healthy, go for a brief 5-minute stroll.

ACTION STEP: Choose a goal. Grab a step to achieving that goal and do one little minuscule task that will move the needle closer to achieving the goal.

The excitement in seeing how close the goal is will be well worth the work.

Target: Focus

Avoid Multitasking

According to a 2009 Stanford research study, multitaskers may appear superhuman, but they pay a high price. Stanford scientists used a group of its undergraduates in the study. They found that half of the undergraduates were media multitaskers while the other half were not.

The multitaskers fared worse on each test, which measured their attention spans, memory capacity, and ability to move from one activity to the next.

In the press release about the findings, a study researcher remarked that the undergraduates were suckers for irrelevancy; anything distracts them.

ACTION STEP: Stick to performing only those objectives for today. Only tackle one task at a time. Focus solely on one aspect of the job and block out everything else.

Practice Meditation

Meditation, which requires a great degree of attention, is a guaranteed technique to improve focus if the adage practice makes perfect is accurate.

Experiments in science back this up. According to research conducted at the University of North Carolina, students who spared 20 minutes of their time daily for four days to meditate fared higher on some cognitive tests.

According to a 2011 study, those who meditated daily were less likely to engage in mind-wandering and were happier overall. Long-term meditators had a reduced level of default mode network activity (DMN), a brain function associated with attention problems, anxiety, and depression.

ACTION STEP: Meditation requires focus. Choose a quote that resonates and is meaningful. Speak this quote over and over out loud. Focus solely on your breath and the repetition. Repeat for at least 20 minutes and longer, if possible.

Exercise Regularly

Running, swimming, and weight lifting is beneficial not just to the body but also to the mind. According to John Ratey, assistant clinical professor of psychiatry at Harvard Medical School, they also improve brain health, which is crucial for memory ability and attention.

Regular exercise, in particular, is thought to assist in the production of a substance called a brain-derived neurotrophic factor, which, according to some studies, aids in the rewiring of memory circuits to increase their performance.

ACTION STEP: Take time to include a workout daily. Whether a 15-minute walk, aerobic circuit training, or dumbbell weight session, make sure to include body movement during the day. It will pay off in a sharper mind and better concentration.

Create A "To-Do" List

To-do lists may help you prioritize which activities need completion first, as well as keep track of any loose ends.

Furthermore, unfinished tasks might detract from your ability to concentrate. The propensity to recall incomplete activities rather than completed ones is also known as The Zeigarnik Effect.

In a 2011 study in the Journal of Economic Behavior and Organization, researchers discovered that participants who could organize their work and complete tasks one at a time were more likely to stay focused than those who jumped from job to task without finishing them.

ACTION STEP: Keep a list of uncompleted tasks or loose ends. Refer to this list daily when time permits to complete each task and get the feeling of accomplishment.

Latte or Matcha?

Sleepy? Try a cup of coffee or a similar caffeinated beverage. Studies indicate that caffeine may aid increased attention in modest quantities, especially in those who are tired. It is advisable to drink no more than 300 mg per day or about 1 1/4 cups of coffee; drinking too much coffee in 24 hours will produce caffeine jitters, sleep disturbances, and more, which causes difficulty concentrating.

If you need a boost at a particular time of day, say 3 p.m., drink coffee at that time and no other. Limiting the quantity of coffee consumed throughout the day will prevent the body from becoming used to the caffeine jolt and produce a smooth concentration boost.

You may also try a cup of tea, which, unlike coffee, will supply you with energy for a longer time due to the L-Theanine molecules included in it, which our systems process throughout the day. L-Theanine can boost mood, lessen physical and mental stress, and improve focus like caffeine. Matcha green tea contains a compound known as EGCG (epigallocatechin gallate) that aids in increased memory.

ACTION STEP: Make a hot or iced cup of coffee or tea every day.

Take Frequent Breaks

Ahhh. The cat videos on YouTube®. Yes, they may help you work more efficiently to some extent. Having a break from work, whether watching cat videos, going for a stroll, or taking a little sleep, is essential.

In one research, 84 people had an hour to complete an easy computer assignment. Those who had two brief breaks throughout that hour performed consistently throughout the hour, but the remaining participants' performance was choppy.

Another well-publicized 2011 study looked at the decision-making process of 1,112 judges and discovered that judges produced more favorable decisions in the morning and after taking periodic meal breaks. This research looked at how semi-frequent pauses helped reduce decision fatigue (i.e., how quickly and correctly we make decisions).

ACTION STEP: Plan to work a manageable amount of time (say 30 minutes) and take a break. Grab some coffee, tea, or snack. Move to a different room and experience a different atmosphere for a bit. It will improve mood and concentration.

Say Yes to Mozart

Ultimately, the right background music is what works for you. Some experts say that listening to no music is ideal for productivity since it reduces distractions.

In comparison to white noise or silence, several types of research have indicated that listening to background music without words improves performance. Another 2005 study showed that the length of a job increased in silence.

Be aware of your productivity and choose tunes that suit you. Magic happens when you pick the right music to listen to while completing a task.

ACTION STEP: Stream music that sets a mood. Research suggests that classical, jazz, movie musicals, and other "no words" music can be beneficial for focus. Be sure to turn this music down low to lessen distraction.

Train The Mental Muscle

Your brain is a mental muscle, and studies have shown that brain training activities like those recommended by Lumosity or Cogmed can help those who are easily distracted.

Although knowing which workouts help and for how long their benefits endure is unclear. As a result, University of California brain and memory researcher Susanne Jaeggi believes further research in brain training is essential.

ACTION STEP: Visit https://www.lumosity.com/en/. Take Lumosity's FREE brain training tests online! These personalized tests help to eliminate brain fog, sharpen your memory and improve your focus. You can take these tests on the go with their app.

Cogmed is another computer-based memory test that incorporates fun video games that helps to improve concentration among other brains exercises.

This testing, however, is done in a clinical setting over a 5-10 week period. A coach will help guide you through each test and provide feedback on the results. Visit their website https://www.cogmed.com/working-memory/get to find a provider in your area.

Stare At A Distant Object

Many of us spend most of our waking hours staring at a computer screen, which can strain our eyes and make it harder to focus.

Look at a distant object for a few minutes to refocus the eyes. Known as the 20-20-20 rule, staring at an object in the distance was prescribed for a journalist at LifeHacker. It works like this: every 20 minutes, take a 20-second glance at anything at least 20 feet away. The concept works since the eye is a muscle that, like all muscles, benefits from exercise. Staring at one thing causes your eyes to feel achy and stiff in the same way that sitting in one location for long periods causes your muscles to feel achy and stiff. Your eyesight might get hazy or fuzzy after work if you fail to refocus regularly.

Blue-light-filtering glasses that block off the blue light emitted by displays have become popular as a way to alleviate screen fatigue; they could improve the quality of your sleep.

ACTION STEP: Take a break and stand at a window. Find the furthest object in the distance and stare at it. Focus solely on that object. Then, look at something close, like the window sill or something near the window. Do this five times.

Sleep Sweetly

One of the most prevalent issues is lack of concentration, a symptom of chronic sleep deprivation. Getting a good seven to eight hours of sleep before a hectic workday may be the difference between being stressed and laser-focused.

ACTION STEP: Before turning in for the night, try the following to help promote deep sleep:

- Make sure the bedroom is not hot(keep temperature between 68 degrees and 74 degrees)
- Make sure the bedroom is dark (purchase room darkening curtains)
- Run an oil diffuser with a pleasant-smelling aromatic oil
- Play soft music with automatic shut off
- Sleep on nylon or silk sheets and pillowcases
- Consider a melatonin supplement.
- Drink chamomile tea before bed.

CONCLUSION

It is easier said than done to learn how to stay focused. Distractions may be found in almost every aspect of our life these days, even if it is just a quick beep from a notification. These types of distractions may appear insignificant, yet anything that takes your attention away from your work can sabotage your productivity.

Avoid distraction. Instead, employ any of the strategies mentioned above to reclaim your concentration and overcome distractions. Your productivity will thank you.

ACTION STEP WORKSHEETS

Veronica Korres

Be Clear on The Vision And Objectives

Make A Vision Board

Grab a cork board or poster board and cut out pictures and words that represent your vision.

Attach them with stapes or push pins or tape.

Keep this vision board in a visible place in your office where you will see it everyday.

Vision Objectives

<u>What do you hope to accomplish through achieving your vision?</u>

I hope to accomplish:

I hope to accomplish:

I hope to accomplish:

Prioritize Your Day

<u>Jot down the 2-3 critical tasks for today.</u>

This must be completed today:

This must be completed today:

This must be completed today:

Target: Focus

Perform Easy Tasks Early

<u>First, Review The Critical Tasks For The Day</u>

What are the easiest parts I can do now?

Do The Bare Minimum

<u>Refer To The Objectives From Vision Board</u>
Break Down The Objectives Into Smaller Goals

Long-Range Goals (Completed In Weeks to Months)

✓	Long-Range Goals

Short-Range Goals (Completed In Less Than A Week)

✓	Short Range Goals

Target: Focus

Avoid Roadblocks

Break down the task at hand into steps.

☆	**Tasks to Complete Today is: (Type the Task Here)**
Step	*Steps to Complete Task: (List Below the Steps to Completing the Task)*
1	
2	
3	
☆	**Tasks to Complete Today is: (Type the Task Here)**
Step	*Steps to Complete Task: (List Below the Steps to Completing the Task)*
1	
2	
3	

Improve Discipline

Method #1:
What Is A Quote That Is Meaningful To You? Write it Here:

Now, Close Your Eyes And Rehearse It Over and Over Silently for 20 Minutes.

Method #2:
1. Locate the timer app on your phone. Set it for 25 minutes.
2. Work the task until the alarm sounds.
3. Take a 5-minute break.
4. Repeat 3 more times.
5. Take a 15 - 30 minute break.

Target: Focus

Keep Your Momentum In Overdrive

1. Never Stop Working Toward Your Goals
2. Keep The Momentum Going By Choose A Goal and Writing Down The Steps To Achieving The Goal.
3. Choose Only One Tiny Task To Perform That Will Bring You Closer To Completion.

☆	**Goal:**
Step	*Steps to Achieve Goal:*
1	
2	
3	
4	
5	

Exercise Regularly

What's Your Favorite Workout?

Choose An Activity And Keep Track In The Chart Below:

Date	Workout Type	Length of Workout

Target: Focus

Create A "To-Do" List

<u>This Will Be A List Of "Loose Ends" That Should Be Handled Today</u>

Date	To-Do List	Completed

Veronica Korres

Thank you for purchasing my book. I would love to know how you liked it!

You can email me at
commentsaboutveronicasbook@yahoo.com

Until next time,
Veronica

Target: Focus

www.ingramcontent.com/pod-product-compliance
Lightning Source LLC
Chambersburg PA
CBHW070852220526
45466CB00005B/1972